APR 0 5 2006

Boueri, Marijean

Lebanon 1-2-3

DUE DATE

Lebanon 1-2-3

A COUNTING BOOK IN THREE LANGUAGES

ENGLISH - FRENCH - ARABIC

Marijean Moran Boueri

Illustrated by Mona Trad Dabaji

PublishingWorks
Exeter, New Hampshire
2005

ACKNOWLEDGMENTS

In particular, Julie Hannouche, who so generously shared her professional knowledge
as well as her keen sense of humor. Special thanks to Joanne Sayad, Jeremy Townsend,
Ellen Feghali, and Randa Karkour. Appreciation to T, C, B, N, E, H, D, J, P, R and K who
encouraged from one to ten.

PublishingWorks
4 Franklin Street
Exeter, New Hampshire 03833

Arabic translation: Caroline Obeid
French translation: Myriam Nguyen

Book Design:
Sally Reed, The Quick Brown Fox, Groton, Massachusetts
Carol Saba, Aleph, Beirut, Lebanon

Printed in Lebanon by Aleph

Library of Congress Cataloging-in-Publication Data

Boueri, Marijean.
    Lebanon 1-2-3 : a counting book in three languages / Marijean Moran Boueri ;
illustrated by Mona Trad Dabaji.
      p. cm.
  In English, Arabic and French.
  ISBN: 1-933002-03-4
1.   Counting--Juvenile literature. 2.   Lebanon--Juvenile literature.   I.
Title: Lebanon one-two-three. II. Dabaji, Mona Trad. III. Title.
  QA113.B666 2005
  513.2'11--dc22
                                    2005049886

To my parents on both continents
Jean and Bob Moran - Rosemary and François Boueri
and to the memory of my grandfather,
John Thomas Batal, M.D. who brought the legendary Lebanese
sense of hospitality with him when he immigrated to America
R E I A F Y O X M

—M.M.B.

A Nayla, Hala, Kassim,
aux enfants qu'ils auront et à tous les autres…
des images, des souvenirs d'enfance
d'un Liban si cher à mon coeur

—M.T.D.

One old house with a red-tiled roof
One balcony broad and breezy

Une ancienne maison au toit de tuiles rouges
Un vaste balcon où souffle la brise

منزل واحد قديم سقفه أحمر من قرميد
شرفة واحدة فسيحة تستقبل النسيم في كلّ حين

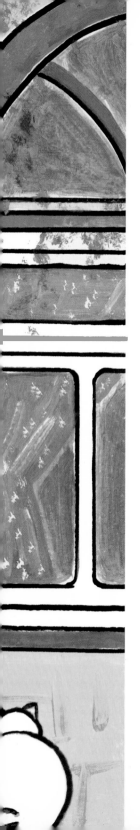

Two doors open wide
Two loving grandparents wait inside

Deux portes s'ouvrent largement
Deux grands-parents attendent joyeusement

درفتان اثنتان مفتوحتان
جدّان محبّان، في الداخل، ينتظران

3

Three welcome kisses for every face
Three graceful arches frame each embrace

Trois baisers accueillent chaque visage
Trois arches encadrent la tendre image

ثلاث قبلات على الوجه للترحيب
ثلاث قناطر جميلة تحضن المتعانقين

٣

4

Four friendly uncles playing cards
Four chairs from France filled with chatting aunts

Quatre oncles jouent aux cartes autour de la table
Quatre tantes bavardent dans leur fauteuil
  si confortable

أربعة أعمام وأخوال ودودين حول الورق مجتمعين
أربعة كراسٍ فرنسيّة الطراز تجلس عليها الخالات والعمّات
للحديث

٤

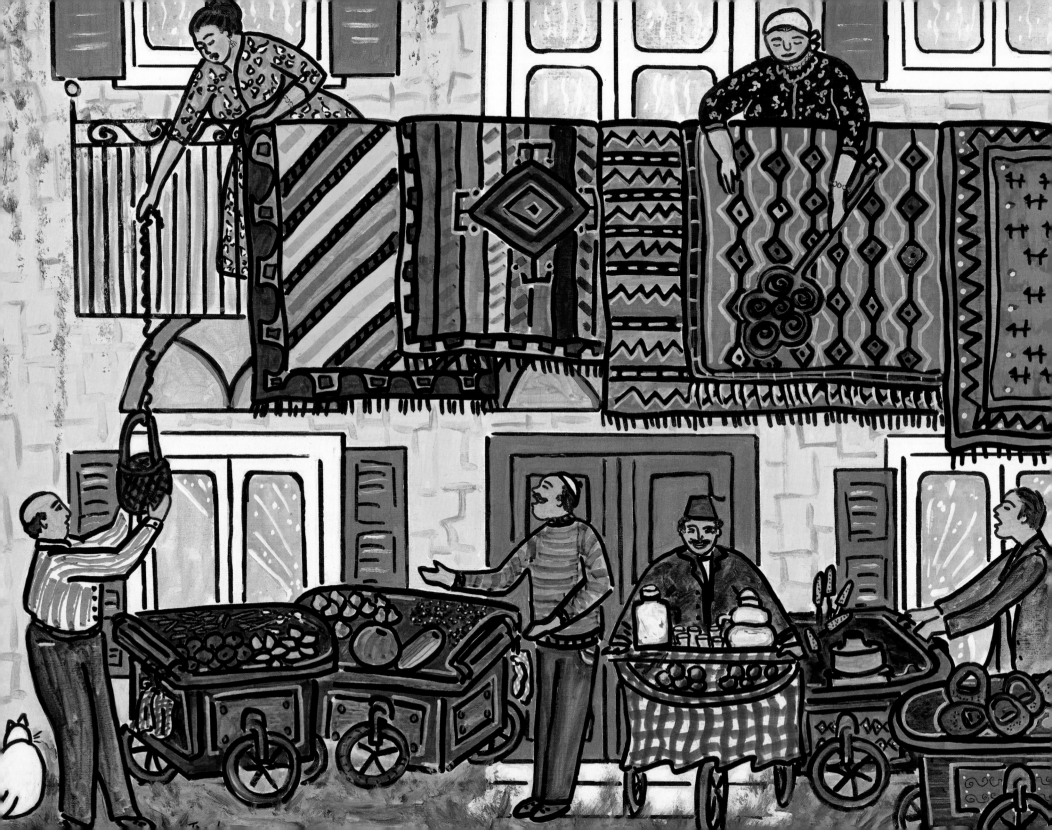

Five peddlers call out with strong voices -
   so many choices!
Five carpets hung in the sun -
   summer has come!

Cinq marchands ambulants crient en passant - que de choix !
Cinq tapis pendent au soleil - l'été est là !

خمسة بائعين متجوّلين بأعلى صوتهم ينادون ـ
فيا للخيارات العديدة
خمس سجادات تحت أشعة الشمس تتدلّى ـ
فها هو الصيف قد حلّ

٥

6

Six confident cooks taste and share
Six savory dishes prepared with care

Six cuisiniers partagent leur festin
Six plats savoureux préparés avec soin

ستّة طهاة ماهرين يتذوّقون ويتبادلون العزيمة على
ستّة أطباق شهيّة حضّروها بكلّ عناية وحنان

٦

Seven silly cousins giggle and grab
Seven syrupy sweets and a feast of fruits

Sept cousins coquins rigolent en saisissant
Sept pâtisseries sirupeuses et des fruits
  rafraîchissants

سبعة أولاد من الأقرباء الأشقياء يتضاحكون ويتماسكون
سبعة أصناف من الحلوى، بالقطر مغمّسة، وتلّة من الفواكه
المنوّعة

8

Eight discs brown and cream remain on the board
  of the backgammon game
Eight beads smooth and round in Uncle's hands
  are often found

Huit pions marrons et blancs sur la table de tric-trac
Huit perles rondes et lisses, entre les mains
  de Tonton glissent

ثمانية أقراص بنية وعاجيّة لاتغادر طاولة النرد
ثماني حبّات مدوّرة ناعمة من مسبحة لا تفارق يد العمّ

٨

9

Nine neighbors gather, young and old
Nine jugs for water, clear and cold

Neuf voisins se rassemblent, grands et petits
Neuf jarres se remplissent d'eau,
 fraîche et limpide

تسعة جيران من كلّ الأعمار مجتمعين
تسعة أوعية بالماء الصافية الباردة مملوءة

٩

Ten birds sing soothing songs that fill the earth and sky
Ten cups of coffee on a tray - so ends this lovely
   Lebanese day !

Dix oiseaux emplissent ciel et terre
   de leur chant rassurant
Dix cafés libanais -
   c'est la fin de cette si belle journée !

عشرة عصافير تغرّد تغريدًا يملأ الدنيا فرحًا

عشرة فناجين من القهوة على صينيّة ـ وبهذا ينتهي يوم

لبناني جميل

Pronouncing Numbers in Arabic and French

The Arabic language is read from right to left. Numbers, however, are read the same way as in English and French, from left to right. Arabic is spoken in many different dialects throughout the world.

Following are the numbers 1-10 in English, French and the way most Lebanese say them:

1	One	*un*	WAH-ad	واحد ١
2	Two	*deux*	T- neyn	إثنان ٢
3	Three	*trois*	TLEIT- eh	ثلاثة ٣
4	Four	*quatre*	AR- baa	أربعة ٤
5	Five	*cinq*	KHAM-seh	خمسة ٥

Did you know that the numerals you use are called Arabic numerals?

English and French speakers use the Arabic numeral system. Arab traders introduced this system to Europe from India. The Arabic numerals were standardized with the invention of the printing press and spread across the world. Today, Arabic numerals are used widely throughout Europe, North and South America, Australia, and various countries in Africa and Asia.

Arabic speakers use the Hindi numeral system.

6	Six	*six*	SIT-tee	ستّة	٦
7	Seven	*sept*	SAB-baa	سبعة	٧
8	Eight	*huit*	T-mey-neh	ثمانية	٨
9	Nine	*neuf*	TIS-saa	تسعة	٩
10	Ten	*dix*	ASH-raa	عشرة	١٠

Can you find...?

ONE
…basket
…fountain
…palm tree
…earring
…bracelet
…amphora: a clay pot with two handles

TWO
…pots of red flowers
…stained glass lights
…protective hands

THREE

…portraits on the wall

…pillows on each couch

…lights for every lamp

FOUR

…cups for coffee

…cards on the table

…bracelets on an aunt

…cards in uncle's hand

…lights on the lamp

…paintings on the wall

FIVE

…cobs of corn

…*kaakat*: the purse-shaped bread

…oranges left and right

SIX

…serving utensils on the table

…plates in each pile

…pots of flowers

SEVEN

…peaches in a bowl

…pastries on a plate

…apricots on a tree

…green figs on a tree

EIGHT

…sunflowers

…flowers in cousin's hand

…colors on the ball

…red figs

NINE

…apples

…neighbors

…jugs for water

TEN

…red flowers

…bunches of purple grapes

…cups of coffee

…birds

About Lebanon

Lebanon is a small but surprisingly diverse country located in the Middle East. The name Lebanon comes from the Arabic word *laban*, which means white, creamy yogurt. In the winter months, snowcapped mountains can be seen from the Mediterranean coast. The Lebanese descend from the Phoenicians, Assyrians, Arabs and Turks. Muslim, Christian and Druze people have been living here together for centuries. Today nearly four million people practice eighteen religions.

Most Lebanese are proficient in the three languages of this book; some even speak a fourth - Armenian. Many families live in apartment buildings in the major cities along the Mediterranean coast: Beirut, the capital city, Sidon and Tripoli. On weekends, these city dwellers escape to their ancestral villages, where time seems to slow down and even the busiest people enjoy the simple pleasures of family, friends, a good meal and nature.